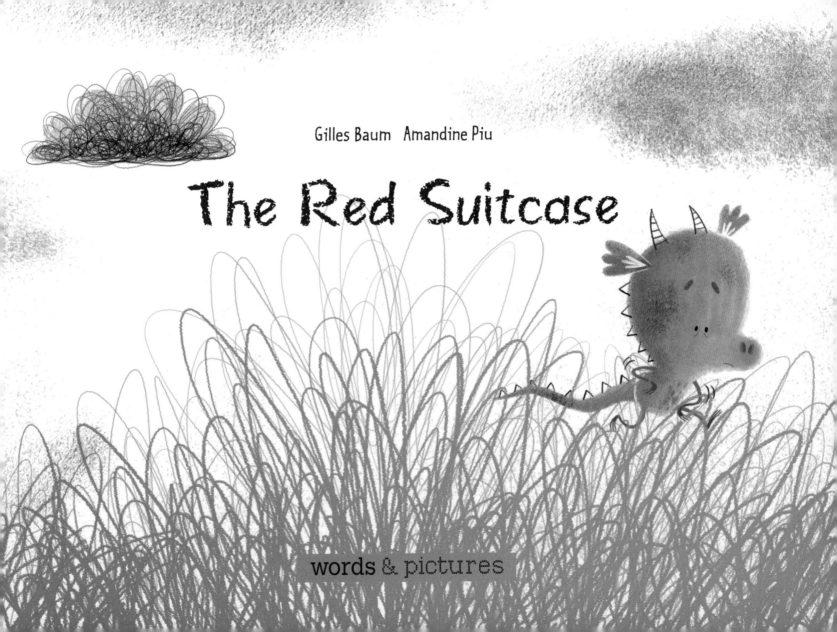

Gilles Baum Amandine Piu

The Red Suitcase

words & pictures

One morning, just go.

Fetch a suitcase, and don't fill it up.

Walk.

Walk faster.

Faster and higher than the clouds.

Smile.

Keep moving forward.

Find a shelter from the rain.

Then keep moving on.

Slide down dunes.

Jump over cliffs.

Regardless of the risks.

Lose yourself in the crowd.

Take a chance.

Cross over the ocean, wave after wave.

Keep your eye on the horizon.

At last, go to sleep under the light of the shining moon.

Far away, yet close. Safe.

The road is still long. Keep going.

Stop. Wait. Be patient.

Have confidence.

Your luck may be just around the corner.

One morning, turn your suitcase into a backpack.

Now keep going. You can go even farther.

Dare. Knock on the door.

Wait for the bell.

Say hello with a big smile.

Tell your story.

And finally, receive something you can't fit in your bag.

A place of safety; a place of joy; a place to belong.